SESAME STREET

Christmas Crafts

First published by Parragon in 2010

Parragon
Queen Street House
4 Queen Street
Bath BA1 1HE, UK

ISBN 978-1-4454-0787-6

Printed in China

123 SESAME STREET®

Christmas Crafts

Parragon
Bath New York Singapore Hong Kong Cologne Delhi Melbourne

TIPS FOR SUCCESS

1

Prepare your space

Cover your workspace with newspaper or a plastic or paper tablecloth. Make sure you and your children are wearing clothes (including shoes!) that you don't mind becoming spattered with food, paint, or glue. But relax! You'll never completely avoid mess; in fact, it's part of the fun!

2

Wash your hands

Wash your hands (and your child's hands) before starting a new project, and clean up as you go along. Clean hands make for clean crafts! Remember to wash hands afterwards too, using soap and warm water to get off any of the remaining materials.

3

Follow steps carefully

Follow each step carefully, and in the sequence in which it appears. We've tested all the projects; we know they work, and we want them to work for you, too. Also, ask your children, if they are old enough, to read along with you as you work through the steps. For a younger child, you can direct her to look at the pictures on the page to try to guess what the next step is.

DID YOU KNOW?
Crafting with children helps to develop their creativity, motor skills, co-ordination, and self-esteem.

4 Measure precisely

If a project gives you measurements, use your ruler, T-square, measuring cups, or measuring spoons to make sure you measure as accurately as you can. Sometimes, the success of the project may depend on it. Also, this is a great opportunity to teach measuring techniques to your child.

5 Be patient

You may need to wait while something bakes or leave paint, glue, or clay to dry, sometimes for a few hours or even overnight. Encourage your child to be patient as well; explain to her why she must wait, and, if possible, find ways to entertain her as you are waiting. For example you can show her how long you have to wait by pointing out the time on a clock.

6 Clean up

When you've finished your project, clean up any mess. Store all the materials together so that they are ready for the next time you want to craft. Ask your child to help.

ADVENT CALENDAR

You will need

- 16 x 23 inch sheet green cardboard
- Sheet of thick white cardboard 10 x 31 inches
- 6 x 8 inch sheet red cardboard
- White glue and brush
- Scrap gold cardboard
- Pencil and rubber
- Scissors
- 23 small empty matchboxes plus one large one
- Silver and red foil gift wrap
- Gold gift ribbon cut into 20 x 24 inch pieces
- Large star sequins
- 25 hard candies or chocolates
- Gold marker pen

1 Kids

Glue the green cardboard to the center of the white cardboard, leaving space at the top and bottom. Cut a star from the gold cardboard and glue it to the top. Cut a pot shape from the red cardboard and glue it as shown. Draw a large Christmas tree shape on the green cardboard and cut the whole shape out.

2

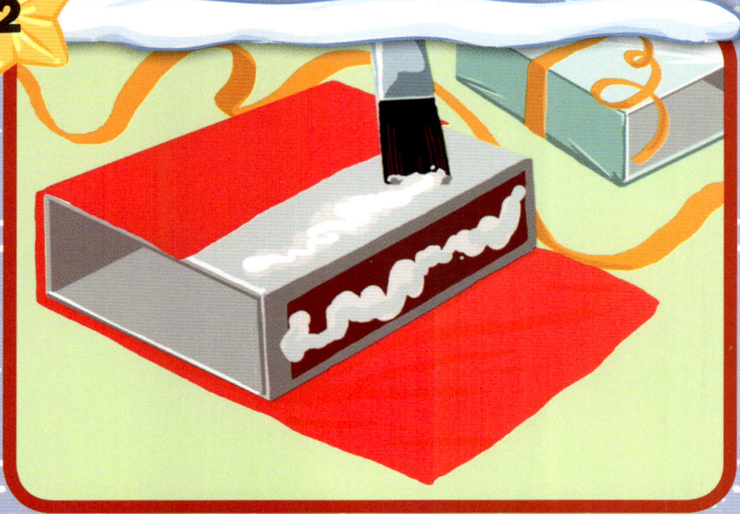

Cover 12 matchboxes in red foil paper and 12 in silver. Tie a length of gift ribbon around each matchbox and tie a double knot in it. Curl the ribbon by pinching it firmly between your thumbnail and index finger and pulling it between them.

3 Kids

Using the gold marker pen, number each of the small boxes from 1 to 23. Write "24" on the big matchbox. Put a wrapped candy or chocolate in each box, and put two in the 24 box.

4

Arrange boxes 1 to 23 randomly on the Christmas tree and put the 24 box in the middle. Glue all the boxes in place. Glue sequin stars onto the tree in the gaps between the boxes.

DID YOU KNOW?

The first advent calendar was made over 200 years ago in Germany.

Elmo's been a very busy monster making this advent calendar. Elmo loves getting a present every day!

REINDEER PUPPET

You will need

- Clean wooden spoon
- Acrylic paint: brown
- Paintbrush
- Brown cardboard
- Brown felt
- Scissors
- White glue
- Two googly eyes
- Small red pom-pom
- Brown wool
- Gold ribbon

1 Kids

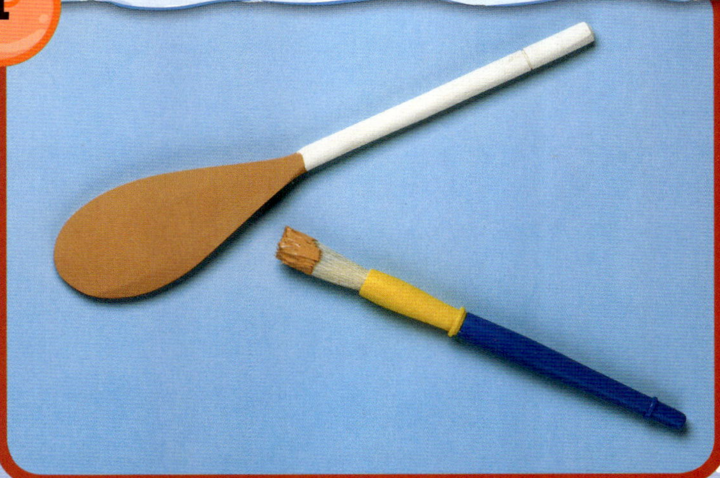

Paint the top of a wooden spoon brown, and let dry.

2

Fold some brown cardboard in half. Draw an antler shape on one side, then cut it out to make two matching antlers. Cut out two felt ears, as shown.

DID YOU KNOW?

"Caribou" is another name for reindeer. Both male and female reindeer have antlers.

3 Kids

Glue the antlers and ears to the back of the spoon, as shown. Then glue the two googly eyes and the red pom-pom nose in place. Let dry.

4

Snip some short lengths of wool, and glue between the antlers to give your reindeer hair. Tie the gold ribbon around the neck to finish your reindeer puppet.

PAPER SNOWFLAKES

You will need

- Small paper plate
- Pencil
- Scissors
- White glue and brush
- Glitter: silver, gold, white
- Thread

1 Kids

Trace around a small plate onto a piece of white paper. Cut out the circle.

2

Fold the circle in half three times, so you end up with a triangle shape. Draw a snowflake pattern along the folded edges of the triangle. Cut out the pattern, making sure you don't cut all the way through the folded edges.

3 Kids

Carefully unfold your snowflake. Cover one side with glue and sprinkle it all over with glitter. Shake off any loose glitter onto scrap paper, and keep it to use for the other side of your snowflake. Let dry.

4

Cover the other side of the snowflake in glue and glitter. When the glue and glitter are completely dry, tie some thread through a hole in the top to hang it up.

DID YOU KNOW?

No two snowflakes are exactly the same, but every real snowflake has six points.

NATIVITY SCENE

You will need

- 2 packs air-drying clay
- Paint: various
- Paintbrushes
- Gold glitter
- Varnish

Kids

1

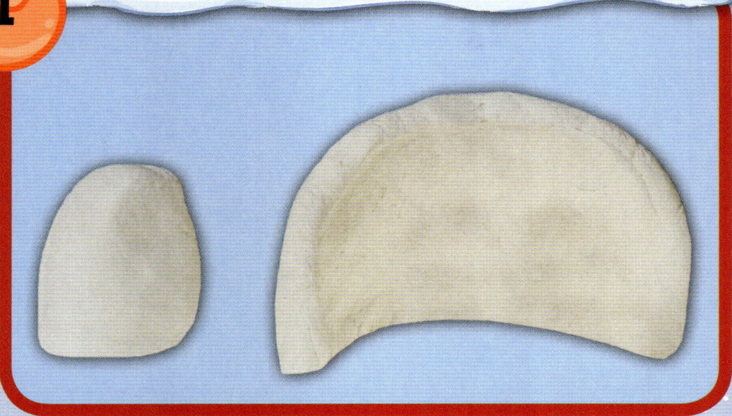

Begin by dividing one pack of clay into two balls, one large, one small. Use the larger ball to shape a curved semicircle for the stable. Make sure the base is flat so it stands up.

2

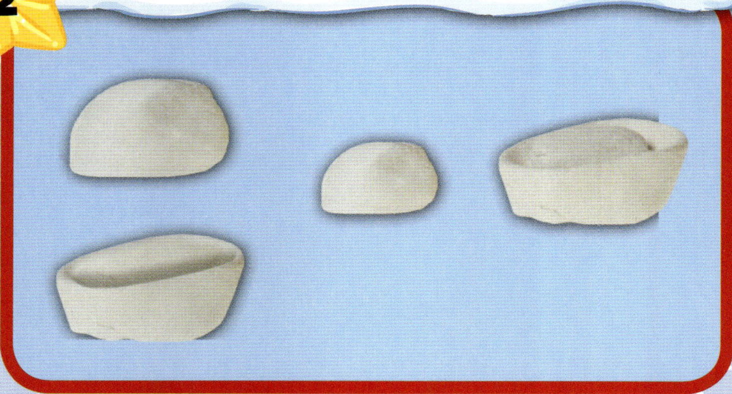

From the second, smaller ball make a small baby's cradle shape—use your fingers to press the base flat. Next make a pebble shape that fits inside the cradle for the Baby Jesus.

3 Kids

Use the second pack of clay to make sausage-shaped figures to be Mary and Joseph. Gently flatten the bases so they stand up. Then make the three kings and shepherds in the same way. Lastly make some pebble shapes for sheep. Let dry according to the clay's instructions.

4

Paint the stable brown and add a white cloth and face on Baby Jesus. Add a face, white robe, and blue cloak to Mary; a green robe and brown headdress to Joseph. Paint the sheep white—add legs and faces. Choose any colors you like for the shepherd and kings' robes and sprinkle glitter onto the kings. Let dry, then varnish. Let dry overnight.

DID YOU KNOW?
You should only add the Baby Jesus to your nativity scene on Christmas Day.

POM-POM SNOWMAN

You will need

- Cardboard toilet-paper tube
- 5 sheets old newspaper
- Cotton batting
- Adhesive tape
- Marker pen
- Glue
- Small black buttons
- Orange felt
- Old, clean sock
- Ribbon

1

Twist some sheets of newspaper as shown, then tape them around the cardboard tube to make the snowman's body.

2

Keep adding layers of newspaper until you have a rounded body shape. Roll a newspaper ball for the head.

3 Kids

Add glue to the head and body, and then cover with the batting.

4 Kids

Glue the head on the body. Glue on a ribbon scarf, two small matching buttons for eyes, and a felt nose.

5

Cut the end off a sock to make a hat to keep your snowman warm. Glue three small matching buttons down his front, and add a friendly smile to finish.

DID YOU KNOW?
The world's biggest snowwoman was built in Maine and was over 122 feet tall.

Make sure you ask a grown-up's permission first, before you cut up any socks!

CHRISTMAS COOKIES

You will need

- Wooden spoon
- Large bowl
- Whisk
- Sieve
- Rolling pin
- Shaped cookie cutters
- Baking sheet
- Cooling rack

- 1 stick butter
- ½ cup sugar
- 1 egg
- 1 teaspoon baking spice
- 1 cup plain flour

Icing and decoration:

- ½ cup confectioner's sugar
- 1 -4 tablespoons hot water
- Tubes of colored icing
- Jimmies to decorate

1

Cream the butter and sugar with a wooden spoon until light and fluffy, then whisk in the egg. Sift in the rest of the ingredients and mix together to make a firm dough. Cover with plastic wrap and chill for two hours.

2

Roll out the dough on a lightly floured surface to about a quarter of an inch thick. Cut out Christmas shapes. Place the shapes onto a greased baking sheet. Bake in a pre-heated oven at 375°F for ten minutes until golden brown.

3 Kids

While the cookies are cooling, mix together the confectioner's sugar with a little hot water and a few drops of food coloring. When cool, ice, then decorate the cookies using jimmies and tubes of colored icing.

4 Kids

When the icing is set, serve the cookies on a plate. Delicious!

DID YOU KNOW?

Traditional German Christmas cookies contain delicious spices such as ginger and cinnamon.

Me love holiday cookies! Num-num!

CHRISTMAS CRACKERS

You will need

- Crêpe paper: green and red
- Cardboard toilet-paper tubes
- Pinking shears
- Jokes on small pieces of paper
- Hard candies in wrappers
- Cracker snaps
- Rubber band
- Sparkly pipe cleaners
- Self adhesive hologram tape
- Small gift bows: red and green

1 Kids

Using pinking shears, cut a piece of green crêpe paper three times as long as the toilet-paper tube and wide enough to go around it with a 1 inch overlap.

2

Put a wrapped candy, folded paper crown, joke and cracker snap in the toilet-paper tube.

3 Kids

Cut red crêpe paper the same width but ¾ inch shorter than the green. Wrap both layers around the tube to hold them in place with a rubber band.

4

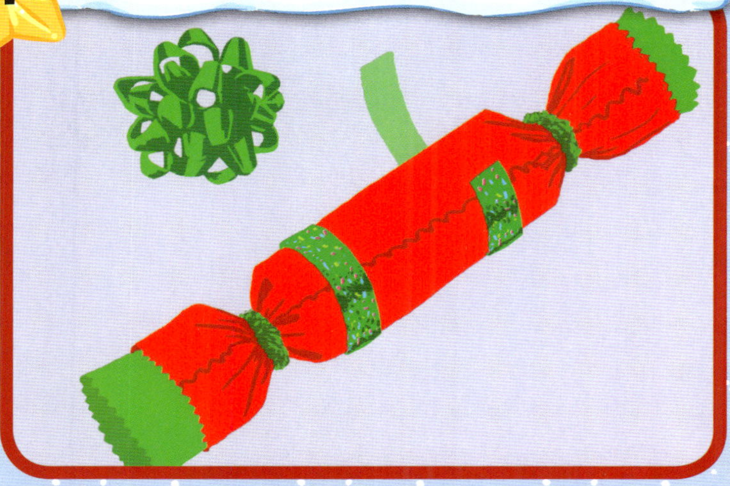

Cut 2 x 6 inch lengths of the pipe cleaners. Twist the ends of the paper and wrap the pipe cleaners around each end of the crackers to keep them closed. Cut 2 strips of hologram tape and stick them around the tube. Remove the rubber band and decorate the tube with a gift bow.

DID YOU KNOW?

When you pull a cracker, the person with the bigger half gets to keep the treats inside.

Paper crowns

It's easy to make paper crowns. Cut a piece of tissue paper about 6 x 24 inches. Glue both ends together and fold it in half twice. Cut the paper to a point. Open it out and you have a crown!

CHRISTMAS TREE CARDS

You will need

- Sheet green paper or thin cardboard
- Black marker pen
- Scissors
- Scraps red paper
- Gluestick
- Colored star sequins
- 3 large gold star sequins

1

Fold the sheet of green paper or cardboard in three, as shown.

2

Draw the outline of a Christmas tree and pot. Make sure the branches run off at the fold or the card will fall apart when you cut it out. Fold the card up and cut the tree out.

Cut three pot shapes from the red paper and glue to the card.

Glue the gold stars to the top of each tree. Add sequins all over the trees to decorate them and let dry.

DID YOU KNOW?
Christmas trees are evergreen. That means they do not lose their leaves, or needles, in winter.

GIFT TAGS

You will need

- Thin, colored cardboard
- Colored construction paper
- Ruler
- Pencil
- Scissors
- Hole punch
- Gluestick
- Ribbon: red, green

1

Measure and cut out some cardboard rectangles six inches by four inches. Fold them in half to make tags, and press along the fold line. Punch holes in the corners, as shown.

2

Draw some shapes for your Christmas decorations onto construction paper and cut them out. Use the hole punch to make lots of circles in different colors from the leftover bits of paper.

DID YOU KNOW?

Holidays are a great time to get in touch with friends and family.

3 Kids

Glue the decorations and hole-punch circles onto the front of the folded tags. Thread ribbon through the holes, so you can attach your tags to gifts.

GIFT BOXES

You will need

- Paper or thin cardboard (letter size will make a box approx. 3 inches square)
- Ruler and pencil
- Scissors
- White glue
- Hole punch
- Colored ribbon
- Double-sided tape
- Self-adhesive stickers

1 Kids

Fold a rectangular piece of paper in half.

2

Fold each half in on itself, so that both ends meet in the middle.

3 Kids

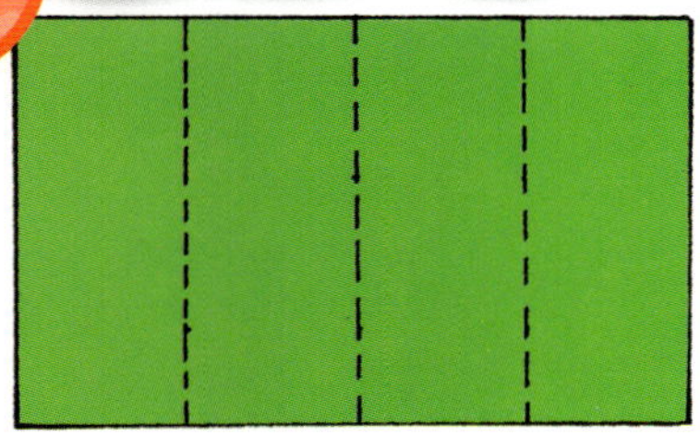

With the paper opened out, you will see crease marks like this.

4 Kids

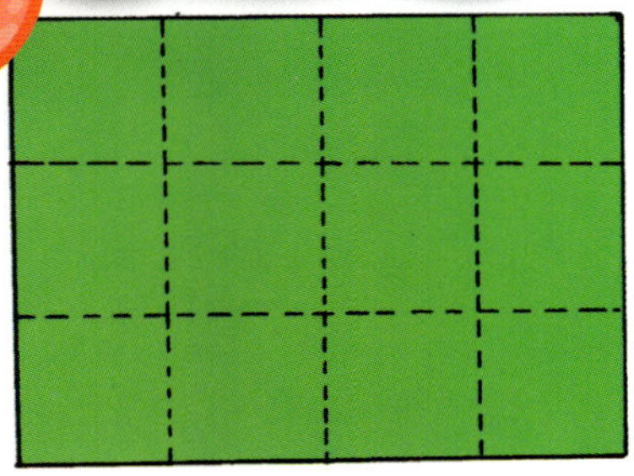

Now fold the paper into thirds in the opposite direction to your first folds. It should look like this picture when you finish with 12 folded squares.

DID YOU KNOW?

The art of folding paper into interesting shapes and objects is called "origami." It comes from Japan.

5

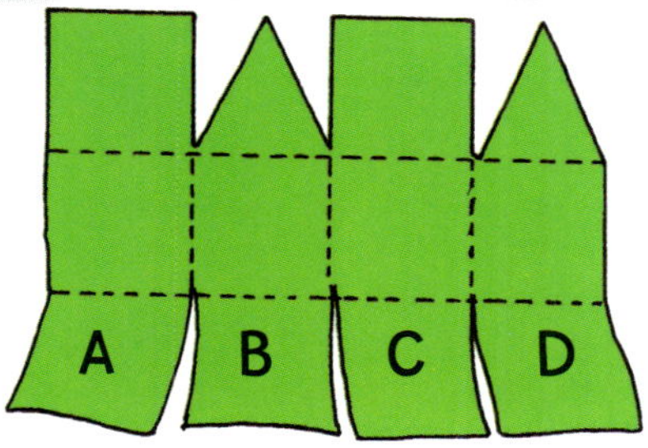

Carefully cut up along the creases marked A, B, C, D in the picture above. Make sure you do not cut beyond the crease of the bottom squares. Then snip off the corners of the top squares of B and D to make triangles as shown above.

6

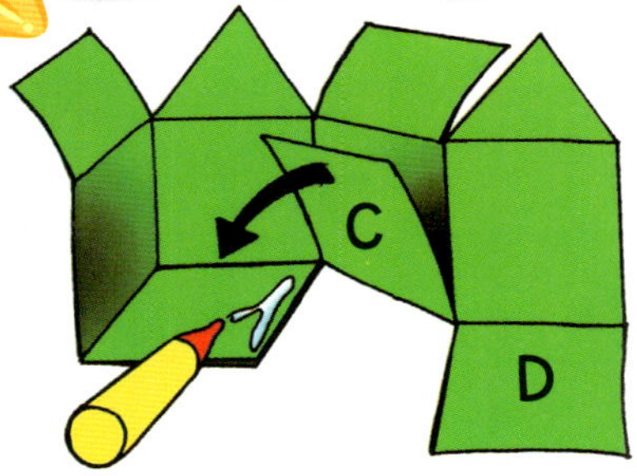

Fold in and glue flap B onto flap A, flap C onto flap B and flap D onto flap C.

7

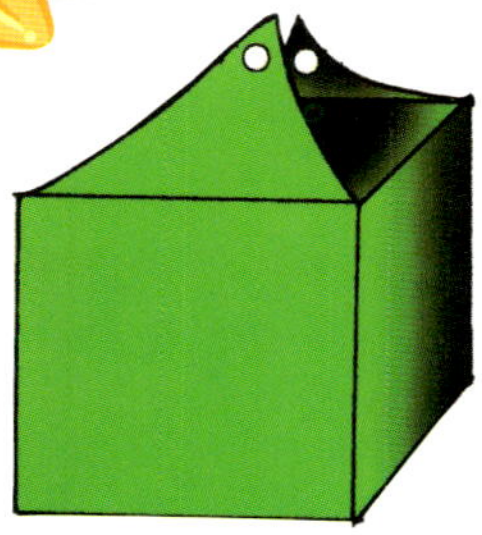

Place double-sided tape on the inside of the open edge to close. Make a hole at the top of both triangles for a ribbon with the hole punch. Decorate your box with the ribbons and stickers.

GIFT WRAP

You will need

- Paper
- Pencil and marker pen
- Scissors
- Tissue paper (to fit gift)
- Paint: gold
- Old saucer
- Sponge
- Hole punch
- Thread
- Clothespins

1

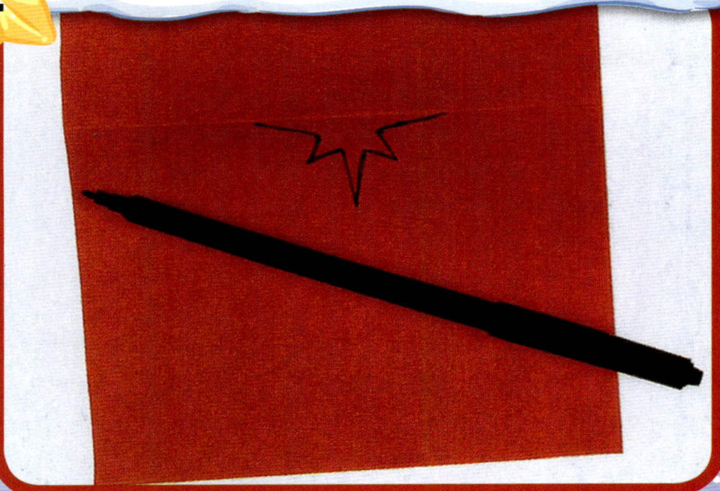

To make a stencil, fold some paper in half and draw half of a star along the fold line, as shown in the picture.

2

Use the scissors to cut the shape out, taking care not to leave any jagged edges. Try not to cut into the paper, too. If you do, the stencil paint may come through.

DID YOU KNOW?
Paper was invented in China thousands of years ago!

3 Kids

Lay out the sheet of tissue paper on a clean work surface. Pour a little paint into a saucer, dip the sponge in, then dab it on paper to get rid of extra paint. Practice stenciling on rough paper, until you are confident.

4

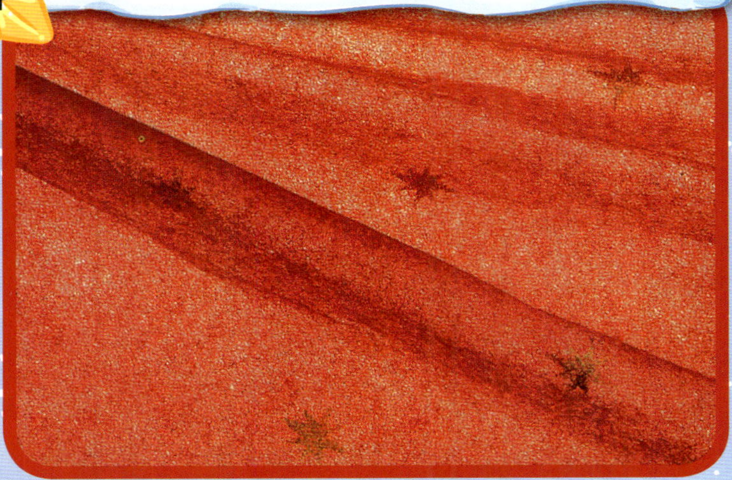

Stencil the shape all over the tissue paper, taking care not to smudge the paint when you lift the stencil off the paper. Hang up your stenciled paper with clothespins on a line to dry. It is a good idea to make a few sheets at a time.

FESTIVE STOCKINGS

You will need

- Thin cardboard
- Marker pen
- Scraps of colored felt
- Scissors
- Ribbon: gold, red
- White glue
- Sequins or craft gems

1

Draw a stocking shape on cardboard and cut it out. Lay the shape on two pieces of felt, then trace around it and cut out two felt shapes.

2

Glue around the edges of the two felt stockings, leaving the top edge unglued so the top stays open. Press the two sides together. Let dry.

DID YOU KNOW?
In some countries, children leave their shoes, not stockings, to be filled with treats.

3

Decorate your stocking with festive felt shapes. Add sequins, gold ribbon, and craft gems for extra sparkle.

4

Glue a loop of red ribbon to the inside of your stocking at the back, so you can hang it up.

Try using glitter on your stocking, too. Sparkalicious!

TREE DECORATIONS

You will need

- Dried pasta shapes: quills and bows
- White glue
- Small wooden balls or beads
- Few grains of rice
- Gold thread
- Gold paint and paintbrush
- Paper or gold tissue paper
- Poppy seedpods
- Scissors

1

Use strong glue to stick the pasta shapes together. Begin with a quill shape, this will be the angel body. A bow shape will make the angel wings, glue this onto the quill.

2 Kids

Glue a wooden ball on as a head and a few grains of rice as hair, and a loop of thread to hang the angel onto the tree. Let dry. Paint gold and let dry thoroughly before hanging on your tree.

DID YOU KNOW?

The modern tradition of decorating Christmas trees began in Germany over 200 years ago.

3

Get some poppy seedpods from a craft store. Carefully cut away the stems so you are left with the pods.

4

Kids

Glue on a loop of gold thread and let dry. Paint gold and let dry thoroughly before hanging on your tree.

INDEX